Respect

By Bruce S. Glassman

With an Introduction by
Michael Josephson,
Founder of CHARACTER COUNTS!ₛₘ

JOSEPHSON
INSTITUTE
CHARACTERCOUNTS!

Produced and created in partnership with Josephson Institute

Special Thanks goes to the following people, whose help on this project was invaluable:

At CHARACTER COUNTS!:
Michael Josephson
Rich Jarc
Amanda Skinner
Mimi Drop
Michelle Del Castillo

Content Advisers:
Dave Bender, book publisher
Tracy Hughes, educator
& CHARACTER COUNTS!
coordinator for Meadowbrook
Middle School, San Diego
Cindy De Clercq, Elementary
School Principal

And thanks to:
Nathan Glassman-Hughes,
Emma Glassman-Hughes,
Natalia Mata, Erica Warren,
Ebony Sanders, Kellen
O'Connell, Nicole Rigler,
and Alex Olberding

Library of Congress Cataloging-in-Publication Data

Glassman, Bruce.
Respect / written by Bruce S. Glassman. — 1st ed.
p. cm. — (Six Pillars of Character series)
Includes bibliographical references and index.
ISBN-13: 978-1-60108-506-1 (hardcover) ; ISBN-10: 1-60108-506-0 (hardcover)
ISBN-13: 978-1-60108-507-8 (pbk.); ISBN-10: 1-60108-507-9 (pbk.)
1. Respect—Juvenile literature. I. Title.

BJ1533.R4G53 2009
179'.9—dc22   2008001190
Printed in China

Contents

Thinking About Character

By Michael Josephson, Founder, CHARACTER COUNTS!

magine that you're taking a big test at the end of the year. You really want to do well on it. You're stuck on a few questions—answers you know will make the difference between a good grade and a possible poor grade. You look up from your test and realize that you can clearly read the answers from the student sitting next to you. You're now faced with a choice. Do you copy the answers or do you go back to staring at your own sheet?

You consider the choices. You know that, if you cheat, you probably won't get caught. And, you think to yourself, copying a few answers is relatively harmless. Who does it hurt? And, besides, everyone does it, right?

Every day you are faced with choices that test your character.

So, what do you do?

Your honest answer to this question will tell you a great deal about your character. Your answer reflects not only what you know is right and wrong, but also how you *act* with what you know.

You are faced with important choices every day. Some choices are "preference choices"—for example, what to wear to school, what to buy for lunch, or what to buy your dad for his birthday. Other choices are "ethical choices." These choices are about what's right and wrong. These are the choices that reflect character.

Ethics play a part in more daily decisions than you may think. The test-taking scenario is only one example of an ethical choice.

You are faced with ethical choices every day. One of the main goals of this series is to show you how to recognize which choices are ethical choices. Another main goal is to show you how to make the right ethical choices.

About Being Ethical

Being ethical isn't simply about what is allowed—or legal—and what is not. You can often find a legal way to do what is unethical. Maybe you saw that a cashier at the grocery store forgot to ring up one of your items. There is no law that says you must tell him or her. But, is it ethical to just walk out without mentioning it? The answer is no. You're still being dishonest by taking something you did not pay for.

So, being ethical is about something more than "what you can get away with." It is about what you do because *you know it's the right thing to do*—regardless of who's watching and regardless of whether you may stand to gain. Often there is a price to pay for doing the right thing.

Character Takes Courage

There are many obstacles to being ethical—chances are you're faced with some of them every day. Maybe you don't want to be

There are many obstacles to being ethical. Overcoming them takes courage and hard work.

embarrassed by telling the truth. Or maybe you feel doing the right thing will take too much effort. Few good things come without a cost. Becoming a person of character is hard work. Here is a poem I wrote that makes this point.

It's Not Easy

Let's be honest. Ethics is not for wimps.

It's not easy being a good person.

It's not easy to be honest when it might be costly, to play fair when others cheat or to keep inconvenient promises.

It's not easy to stand up for our beliefs and still respect differing viewpoints.

It's not easy to control powerful impulses, to be accountable for our attitudes and actions, to tackle unpleasant tasks or to sacrifice the now for later.

It's not easy to bear criticism and learn from it without getting angry, to take advice or to admit error.

It's not easy to really feel genuine remorse and apologize sincerely, or to accept an apology graciously and truly forgive.

It's not easy to stop feeling like a victim, to resist cynicism and to make the best of every situation.

It's not easy to be consistently kind, to think of others first, to judge generously, to give the benefit of the doubt.

It's not easy to be grateful or to give without concern for reward or gratitude.

It's not easy to fail and still keep trying, to learn from failure, to risk failing again, to start over, to lose with grace or to be glad for the success of another.

It's not easy to avoid excuses and rationalizations or to resist temptations.

No, being a person of character is not easy.

That's why it's such a lofty goal and an admirable achievement.

Character Is Worth It!

I sincerely hope that you will learn and use the ideas of CHARACTER COUNTS! The books in this series will show you the core values (the Six Pillars) of good character. These values will help you in all aspects of your life—and for many years to come. I encourage you to use these ideas as a kind of "guide-rail" on your journey to adulthood. With "guide-rails," your journey is more likely to bring you to a place where you can be a truly good, happy, and ethical person.

Michael Josephson
Founder of Josephson Institute and CHARACTER COUNTS!

chapter 1

What Is Respect?

What do you think of when you think of respect?

Do you think about being polite to someone? Minding your manners? Obeying authority?

These are some ways that you can be respectful. But the idea of respect is more than just being polite. A person of good character has a basic respect for himself and every other human being. This kind of respect recognizes that all people—no matter who they are or what they have done—are entitled to basic human dignity.

Being respectful of everyone else does not mean you need to hold everyone in high esteem, or admire them. But it does mean

Respect means recognizing that all people are entitled to basic human dignity.

you recognize that all human beings deserve respect as a basic part of their existence.

The 7 Guidelines of Respect

There are seven basic rules to follow in order to be truly respectful.

They are:

1. Honor the individual worth and dignity of others

2. Live by the Golden Rule ("Do Unto Others As You Would Have Them Do Unto You")

3. Show courtesy and civility

4. Be tolerant of differences in others and judge them on their character and ability

5. Allow others to make their own choices and have free will

6. Honor reasonable social standards and customs

7. Avoid actual or threatened violence

Respect is the foundation of friendship and love.

Honoring the Worth of Others

People are not things. Every human being has a right to be treated with dignity. The right to dignity is part of being human. It has nothing to do with how rich a person is. Or what job they hold. Or what they may be able to do for you.

Respect for basic human dignity is a key part of America's democracy. The very founding of our nation was based on the idea that all people "are created equal."

The Framers of our Constitution thought respect and human dignity were very important. They made sure the concept of basic human rights was a key part of the Constitution.

The U.S. Constitution honors respect for basic human dignity.

Before the Constitution, Thomas Jefferson wrote the Declaration of Independence. Jefferson also included many key ideas about human rights and dignity. The following is the first major idea set forth by the Declaration:

> *We hold these truths to be self-evident, that all men are created equal, that they are endowed by their Creator with certain unalienable Rights, that among these are Life, Liberty and the pursuit of Happiness.*

Amnesty International

Many organizations around the world work to protect human rights. One of the largest and most famous is called Amnesty International. AI has more than 2.2 million members from more than 150 countries around the world.

AI's core mission is to force governments that abuse human rights to change their ways. In many of these countries, citizens are not allowed freedom of expression or the right to vote.

AI uses its Universal Declaration of Human Rights to govern itself. This declaration contains 30 Articles, each of which makes a statement about human rights. Here are excerpts from the Declaration of Human Rights, which was adopted in 1948:

In Afghanistan, the Taliban did not allow women to work.

ARTICLE 1: All human beings are born free and equal in dignity and rights. They are endowed with reason and conscience and should act towards each other in a spirit of brotherhood.

ARTICLE 2: Everyone is entitled to the rights and freedoms set forth in this Declaration, without distinction of any kind, such as race, color, sex, language, religion, political or other opinion, national or social origin, property, birth, or other status.

ARTICLE 3: Everyone has the right to life, liberty, and security of person.

Amnesty International has been one of the most effective human rights organizations in the world. It is also one of the best known. Among its many members are Hollywood celebrities, musicians, and artists. Some of the celebrities who support AI include Aerosmith, Christina Aguilera, Coldplay, Corinne Bailey Rae, Green Day, Jennifer Lopez, Lenny Kravitz, Robin Williams, Sting, and U2.

You can find more about Amnesty International at www.amnesty.org

Lenny Kravitz (left) and Green Day (above) are some of AI's famous members.

Living by the Golden Rule

"Do unto others as you would have them do unto you." This is the second basic rule for being respectful. If you follow it, you won't treat anyone else in a way you wouldn't want to be treated.

Aristotle

Around 350 B.C.E., the Greek philosopher, Aristotle, said "We should behave to others as we wish others to behave to us." He wasn't the first one to say that. But that idea came to be known as The Golden Rule. It is almost universally accepted. Most major religions of the world have some version of the Golden Rule in their teachings (see sidebar, page 19).

The Golden Rule is so useful, you can use it to think about any action you may take. With regard to building character, you can always ask yourself, "Would it be good if everyone in the world made this choice?" "What if I were on the other end of this decision?"

Showing Courtesy and Civility

Do you remember, when you were younger, how everyone taught you the importance of saying "Please" and "Thank you"? It may have seemed like everyone was making a big deal over something relatively small. But manners and courtesy are not small things. When we interact with other people, courtesy shows others that we respect them enough to be mindful of how we act.

Do you notice how good you feel when someone is courteous to you? The simple act of hearing someone say "thank you" or "excuse me," makes you feel acknowledged and appreciated.

We are often asked to show respect not only to people, but also to certain things. These special things are usually symbols that have great meaning in our culture: The American Flag. The National Anthem. A headstone at a gravesite. A crucifix. These are examples of things that hold great meaning to many people. We are often asked to show our respect to those things—even if those things are not of great importance to us personally. Here's a good example of respect for a symbol:

Showing courtesy to others is a key part of being respectful.

In 1960, John F. Kennedy (JFK) was elected president of the United States. Kennedy was young and good-looking, had great charm, and was very diplomatic. Many people credit JFK's election victory, however, to another man: his brother Bobby.

Bobby Kennedy was John's campaign manager and his closest adviser. No one had access to JFK the way Bobby did. When John became president, he named Bobby attorney general of the United States.

Working so closely together in White House, the two brothers often had to speak about each other in public. When they did, however, they referred to each other only by their respective titles. John referred to "the attorney general" and Bobby referred to "the president."

Why did two men who were so close—who were family—speak so formally about each other in public? They did it to show respect for what each represented. John and Bobby were more than just men, or brothers. They were symbols of things that were very important to every American. Bobby was the country's highest-ranking lawyer—the president's legal counsel. John was the president of the United States—the leader of the nation.

The Golden Rule in Religions

From left: Mosque, Christian Church, Jewish Temple

Most major world religions include some version of the Golden Rule in their teachings. Here are some examples:

CONFUCIUS: "What you do not want done to yourself, do not do unto others."

JUDAISM: "What you dislike for yourself, do not do to anyone."

CHRISTIANITY: "Do unto others as you would have them do unto you."

ISLAM: "No one of you is a believer unless he loves for his brother what he loves for himself."

HINDUISM: "Do nothing to thy neighbor which thou wouldst not have him do unto thee thereafter."

BUDDHISM: "Hurt not others with that which pains thyself."

Being Tolerant of Differences in Others

Every person has a unique identity. An identity is usually a mix of things from different areas of our lives. It can come in part from dressing a certain way. Or belonging to a certain sports team, religion, or club. It can also come from things we cannot choose for ourselves, such as body type, height, how you speak, or whether you can walk, see, or hear.

Helen Keller was blind, deaf, and unable to speak from childhood. She said, "The highest result of education is tolerance." Helen Keller was saying that, the more a person is exposed to, the more tolerant she is likely to be. William Hazlitt, an English writer, agreed. He wrote,

Being respectful means being tolerant of those different from you.

"Prejudice is the child of ignorance." In fact, the word *prejudice* means "to make a decision before you have all the necessary information." In other words, to *pre-judge.* When you pre-judge, you make a decision based on ignorance.

Being respectful of others means being tolerant of their identities. It also means accepting identities that are different from yours.

Another part of being tolerant is avoiding what are called "snap judgments." These are judgments based on superficial things, such as the clothes someone is wearing, or the color of their skin. When you avoid judging people on the superficial things, you are showing respect. You are respecting the idea that others should be judged on their actions, not on the hat they wear or the neighborhood in which they live.

Have you ever thought about what the world would be like if everyone was more tolerant? Unfortunately, lack of tolerance is one of the biggest causes of violence and hate in the world. There is intolerance of different religions. There is intolerance of different ethnic backgrounds and skin colors. There is intolerance based on gender. These are some of the most common causes of hate. How common is hate in our world? According to an organization called Tolerance.org, a crime motivated by hate is committed every hour of every day in America. They also report that every day at least 8 blacks, 3 whites, 3 Jews, and 1 Latino become victims of a hate crime.

Ways You Can Fight Hate

Tolerance.org is one of many agencies that works to increase tolerance in the world. It has published a pamphlet called "10 Ways to Fight Hate." Here is a summary of some of their main ideas:

1. TAKE ACTION. If you witness or experience intolerance or hatred, do something. Speak out. Silence or lack of action can be taken for acceptance.

2. BE A GOOD EXAMPLE. The best way to spread tolerance is to show it. When others see you being kind, fair, and tolerant they will be more likely to follow.

3. DIG DEEPER. Look inside yourself and work to shed your own prejudices and bias.

A hate crime at a synagogue

Have you ever pre-judged some-one unfairly? Have you ever made assumptions about someone that you found were wrong?

Learn more about Tolerance.org by visiting their web site.

Letting Others Have Control of Their Lives

Another part of respect is recognizing that other people should be free to make their own choices. Respect requires us to honor the right of all people to have control over their own lives. All people, including kids, should have some say in the decisions that affect them.

Deciding how you will act and making your own choices is also called free will. The use of free will is a kind of independence. It is part of what makes us feel in control of our lives. This control gives us a stronger sense that we all have basic human rights. It also gives us a feeling of self worth.

Free will and independence do not mean doing whatever you want. For example, we cannot allow people in our society to use their free will to cause violence or destruction. Parents cannot allow growing children to use their free will without limits. Part of parenting is guiding and showing kids what the right choices are—especially when the kids don't recognize those choices. Kids earn their use of free will by showing they can use it wisely.

Honoring Reasonable Social Standards

This basic rule is about respecting the culture you are in. In our society, we have codes of conduct and certain expectations of proper behavior. Different people may interpret these codes differently. Most of the time, the expectations are about dressing appropriately, speaking

Social standards are the expectations of proper behavior and dress.

appropriately, and acting in a manner that is appropriate for the context (your surroundings). So, what does all that mean? Well, here's an example of context: There's nothing wrong with wearing a bathing suit to the beach, right? But how about wearing just your board shorts or bikini to a church, mosque, or synagogue? Or a funeral? Attire like that is inappropriate in those contexts.

Just like education breeds tolerance, it also breeds respect. If you are going to be exposed to a culture other than yours, you will be more able to be respectful if you know something about that culture. In some cases, what you think is respectful may actually be insulting in another culture (see sidebar).

Avoiding Violence

As you may have noticed, all the basic rules of respect are related to one another in some way. The final basic rule of respect—avoiding violence—is particularly tied to the ideas we have already discussed: Every person is entitled basic human rights, the right to use free will, the right to be accepted and tolerated, and the right to feel safe.

The use of violence—or the threat of violence—prevents other people from enjoying their basic human rights. And that means they are not being treated with respect.

Most kids learn from an early age that violence against other people is not acceptable. They learn that as part of how to be respectful of others. Learning to control the urge to hit or bully is one of the most difficult things a child must do. For many people, the urge to be violent never completely goes away—even as an adult. Responsible and respectful adults, however, have learned how to control those urges.

Bullying Is Not Respectful

Bullying is the most common form of violence in American schools today. According to the Bullies Beware organization, a student is bullied in America every 7 seconds. Bullying happens in a number of ways. Sometimes it is done with physical violence or the threat of physical violence. Other times it is indirect, such as isolating someone from a group or ignoring them. Other times bullying can be more emotional, such as making another person feel ashamed or disrespected. Still other times, the bullying can be verbal: a bully may hurl insults or say or write mean and hurtful things.

Bullying—no mater what kind—is unacceptable behavior. Many people think that the best way to deal with a bully is to ignore him or

Learn About Some Other Cultures

In America, if you are invited to someone's house for dinner, you might bring flowers to your hosts, right? In Egypt, however, your hosts would not want flowers. In Egypt, flowers are reserved for weddings or people who are ill. In Russia, male guests are actually expected to bring flowers, but not yellow flowers. If you're in Brazil, don't bring purple flowers—purple is the color of mourning in Brazil. In India, white flowers are used at funerals.

Here is a brief look at some of the other fascinating differences among cultures of the world.*

You'll see that other cultures have very different beliefs and traditions from those you may already know. To learn about other cultures is to better understand them. And understanding them is the first step to accepting and respecting them.

MEETING AND GREETING:

• In China, a handshake is usually light. During a greeting, a Chinese person may lower their eyes as a sign of respect.

• In Egypt, handshakes are somewhat limp and prolonged. They are always accompanied by a hearty smile and direct eye contact.

• In India, a man may shake hands with another man, and a woman may shake with another woman, but a man will rarely shake hands with a woman.

GIVING GIFTS:

• In Brazil, you do not give a handkerchief as a gift because it is associated with death and funerals.

*Information provided by kwintessential.co.uk

• In Egypt, a person must always give a gift with the right hand.

• In India, a Hindu should not be given a gift made of leather. A Muslim should not be given alcoholic products or a gift made of pigskin.

• In China, clocks, handkerchiefs, and straw sandals are associated with funerals and death. They should be avoided as gifts. Other gifts to avoid include scissors, knives, or other cutting utensils. These things signify that you want to "sever"—or cut—the relationship. In China, a person never offers anything in the quantity of four. The quantity of eight is considered very good.

• In Brazil, gifts are opened when received. In China, India, and Egypt, gifts are not opened when received.

DINING AND TABLE MANNERS:

• In Egypt, it is considered an insult to salt your food.

Different cultures have varied customs for flowers.

• In China, burping at the table is considered a compliment.

• Hindus and Sikhs do not eat beef. Muslims do not eat pork or drink alcohol.

• In India, China, Russia, and Egypt, it is considered polite to leave some food on your plate. This shows your hosts that you are satisfied and that they have provided more than enough hospitality.

Avoiding the use of violence is one of the most basic rules of respect.

her. This is not true. If you witness bullying, or are a victim of it, you should do whatever you can to stop it. This does not mean do it on your own. Parents, teachers, and community leaders can all help. The important thing is to take action.

Think about bullying and what you have learned about respect. Does bullying:

1. Honor the individual worth and dignity of others?
2. Stand up to the Golden Rule (Do Unto Others As You Would Have Them Do Unto You)?
3. Show courtesy and civility?
4. Show tolerance of differences in others?
5. Allow others to make their own choices and have free will?
6. Honor reasonable social standards and customs?

TAKE A BULLYING QUIZ: How Much Do You Know?

On a separate sheet of paper, answer each question with a "T" for true or an "F" for false. [Answers are upside down at the bottom.]

#1: Only boys bully. _____

#2: Bullies have low self-esteem. _____

#3: Bullies can be smaller than their victims, and less physically strong. _____

#4: The best way to stand up to a bully is to fight back. _____

#5: Bullying can happen anywhere. _____

ANSWERS:

F. [Many girls are bullies, too.]

F. [Bullies may suffer from other feelings of neglect or frustration, but lack of self-esteem is not the issue.]

T. [Remember, there are many kinds of bullying, including emotional, verbal, and cyberbullying (see sidebar). These forms have nothing to do with physical size.]

F. [Fighting back only confirms to the bully that physical violence is the answer to solving problems.]

T. [Bullying can happen in school, on your sports team, walking through your neighborhood, even through email and text messaging.]

Cyberbullying

The problem of bullying is as old as human civilization. Unfortunately, as new technologies evolve, so do ways to bully. Cell phones, text messaging, web sites, and other technologies are nearly everywhere, and so is bullying. A relatively new form of bullying— called cyberbullying—is a growing concern.

Cyberbullying is when one child targets another through interactive technologies; cell phones, text messaging, web sites, instant messaging, or interactive games. The bullying can be in the form of a hateful message. It can be anonymous or signed. It can be a nasty web site, where, for example, other kids vote for the "ugliest, fattest, or stupidest" kids in school.

Bullying can also be a death threat sent anonymously or posted online. It can be password theft, where a bully will lock a victim out of an account, or share the password with others. A cyberbully may hack into a victim's computer to send viruses, rack up charges, or send vital information to other people who will do harm.

The statistics on the growth of cyberbullying are alarming. Michele Ybarra is an internet researcher and web site creator. She estimates that 1 in 4 teens are cyberbullies. Another 1 in 4 teens said they have been cyberbullied at least once. Another organization that promotes Web safety, I-Safe America, surveyed 1,500 students in 4th through 8th grade. 42% of them

Cyberbullying has become a major problem in America.

said they have been bullied online. 53% of them admitted to saying something mean or hurtful to someone else online. Sometimes the bullies cause little damage, but other times the bullying can become very serious. Numerous victims of cyberbullying have committed suicide.

The technologies that we live with everyday have changed the face of bullies. In fact, they have removed the faces of bullies in many cases. Before the internet, most bullies were known to their victims. Often, the bullying was physical and was only done in person. Cyberbullies, however, can hurt others anonymously. And they can do it regardless of their size, gender, age, or other physical characteristics.

For more information about cyberbullying, check out these web sites:

www.stopcyberbullying.org
www.Cyberbully411.org
www.cyberbullying.us

chapter 2

The Importance of Respect

A desire for respect and basic human rights has been at the center of many struggles throughout history. A lack of respect—a lack of tolerance and acceptance—has also played a key role in many of the world's most violent and destructive conflicts.

Intolerance in the World Today

Unfortunately, a lack of tolerance and acceptance can be blamed for many of the worst conflicts we see today. In some countries,

In 2007, protestors filled the streets of Jena, Louisiana, where racial violence at a high school became headline news. ❯

intolerance and hatred between groups goes back hundreds—even thousands –of years. This kind of long-term intolerance creates deep hatred. Too often, this hatred leads to violence.

In Iraq, for example, tens of thousands have been killed in violence between Sunni Muslims and Shiite Muslims. These two branches of Islam have been in conflict ever since the death of Muhammad (the founder of Islam) in A.D. 632. When Muhammad died, the Sunnis believed Muhammad's father-in-law should take his place. The Shiites believed Muhammad's cousin should be the successor. This disagreement has caused centuries of hatred, conflict, and violence from both sides.

In recent years, the conflict between Sunnis and Shiites has created a civil war in Iraq. Both sides want to limit the power and influence of the other. Neither side wants the other to have a hand in government or community life. This bitter conflict has prevented the country from forming an effective and stable government.

Think about your community, your town, or your city. Do you see intolerance? If so, how does it affect people? How does it affect different parts of daily life?

Violence between Sunni and Shiite Muslims has gone on for centuries.

A Historical Look at Respect

A great deal of America's history is tied to a search for tolerance. Many times, our nation's history has been shaped by a search for religious tolerance and freedom.

Roger Williams was a Puritan minister who arrived in America in 1631. He sailed from his native England in search of a land that would be more tolerant of new and different religious views. The Church of England was very rigid and did not tolerate freedom of ideas.

Roger Williams believed people should have freedom of opinion on religious matters—something he called "soul liberty." He also felt strongly that there should be a "wall of separation" between religion and other matters of government, law, and society.

While serving as a minister in Massachusetts's Plymouth colony, Williams developed a deep friendship with—and respect for—the Native Americans of the area. He believed that the Native Americans should be treated as equals.

Despite his own strong religious beliefs, Roger Williams was opposed to forcing Christianity on the Native Americans. Many European settlers felt it was their mission to convert non-Christians. Often, their conversion methods used violence, torture, or the threat of both. Williams felt that forced conversion was "monstrous and most inhumane." He also believed that forcing others to change their beliefs was a "violation of Christian principles."

Williams earned the trust and respect of Native American leaders. He then helped to protect their rights and to negotiate between the white settlers and various tribes. Williams spent a good deal of time actually living with Native Americans. He ate with them, slept in their camps, and learned their language.

Roger Williams

Williams eventually journeyed to the present-day site of Providence, Rhode Island. With twelve fellow settlers, he secured land from the local Native Americans and established a settlement of his own. Williams wanted his colony to be based on the principle of equality. The somewhat unique system of government they created allowed for a separation of religion and civil matters. This idea was admired and later adopted by Thomas Jefferson and America's Founders.

In 1643, the citizens of the growing colony—formally named "Providence"—sent Williams to England to secure a charter. By 1647, the original Rhode Island colony was united with Providence under a single government. When they came together, the colony was once again officially proclaimed to be a safe haven for all people who were persecuted or punished for their beliefs. Everyone and anyone was welcome—Baptists, Jews, even Quakers, who were being persecuted and killed in Massachusetts. All citizens in Rhode Island

The Rhode Island colony succeeded largely because Roger Williams built trust and friendship with the Native Americans of the region.

were allowed to follow their own consciences in peace and safety. On May 18th, 1652, Rhode Island passed the first law in North America making slavery illegal.

The Rhode Island colony respected people of all faiths. By 1639, the first Baptist churches in America had been founded by Roger Williams and John Clarke. By 1759, Newport had the establishment of the Touro Synagogue, the first synagogue in North America.

Roger Williams's vision enabled people from all backgrounds and beliefs to come together for a common purpose. In doing that, the people of Rhode Island not only looked out for each other, they also promoted the values of tolerance and respect. These values later provided an important foundation for the government we would come to know as the United States. To this day, the state of Rhode Island—especially the city of Providence—proudly maintains its tradition of equality and respect for everyone.

chapter 3

Respect in Your Life

O n a personal level, respect plays an important role in many areas of your life. It is important in two primary ways: The respect you give, and the respect you get. These two kinds of respect affect each other. The more respect you show to others, the more respect you will get in return.

The Respect You Give

Think about all the things you are asked to do in order to show respect. You are asked to address your parents in a way that shows them respect. The same goes for the way you address your teachers, your coaches, and other adults in your community. You are also expected to respect flags, religious icons, statues, and other things that symbolize

The more respect you show to others, the more you will get in return. ❯

Flags are important symbols.

ideas or beliefs that are important to people. These expectations of respect are taught to you as you grow up. They are behaviors that your family, your community, and your country ask of you.

When the entire crowd at a baseball stadium rises and takes off their hats for the "National Anthem," they are not only showing respect for the flag and the song, but also showing respect for America itself. As the anthem is sung, everyone in the stadium shows and shares respect at the same time. Shared respect for a common idea is a bond that unites people of a country to a common purpose.

Being respectful does not mean simply going along with what everyone else expects. Many people have good reasons to disobey expectations of behavior in order to protest certain policies or actions. As long as protests are respectful of others, they may be effective ways to show your opinions.

What if you are asked to show respect for something you don't believe in? Here's an example about respect to consider:

> David and Keith are 13-year-olds who have known each other since they were infants. Their parents are best friends, and they have lived near each other all

their lives. David is Jewish and Keith is Protestant. Their faiths are important to each of them. Because they love and respect each other as best friends, they have each learned a great deal about the other's religion.

When it came time for Keith to have his Confirmation, David and his family were invited. As Keith's best friend, David was asked to sit in the front row with Keith's parents, grandparents, aunts, uncles, and cousins. The ceremony began and David started to panic. He had never actually been in a church service before. He realized that the reverend was speaking a lot about God, and specifically about Jesus Christ being the Lord. Many times, the entire church would read aloud in unison from the prayer book.

David decided that he could not read along with the prayers in the book, since he did not believe them. He also decided, when the congregation said "Amen" to confirm a prayer, he would remain silent. Instead, he stood quietly, head bowed, and listened. When the ceremony was over, David was very worried that he had offended Keith and his family by not participating.

What do you think? Was David disrespectful?

Kids Can Make a Difference

Zach Hunter is only 15 years old, but he's already a worldwide champion of human rights.

When he was only in the 7th grade, Zach founded an organization in his hometown of Atlanta, Georgia, called Loose Change to Loosen Chains. Its goal is to encourage students to donate spare change to groups that work to end human rights abuses.

So far, Zach has personally raised $20,000 to help free slaves around the world. More than 30 schools now support his cause.

Find out more about Loose Change to Loosen Chains at: www.lc2lc.org

The Respect You Get

All people want respect. The desire to be respected is a basic human need. When you feel respected, you feel you have worth, dignity, and identity. Feeling these things brings happiness. And happiness is something everyone works toward.

As much as you should demand respect of yourself toward others, you should also insist on respect from others. If you feel someone else is not treating you with respect, you need to take action. You need to make it clear that disrespect is unacceptable. You may feel comfortable dealing with the problem alone. But it may be an issue that you need help addressing. If that's the case, you should seek out a parent, a counselor, or other individual who can help.

Learning How to Make Good Choices

A famous lawyer and speechmaker named William Jennings Bryan once said, "Destiny is not a matter of chance, it is a matter of choice." He was saying that we have more control over our lives than we often assume.

More than anything else, your life will be affected by the choices you make. Knowing how to make good choices is most often the difference between being happy and being miserable.

Two Core Principles of Choice-Making

There are two fundamental principles that form the foundation of good decision-making. They are:

1. We all have the power to decide what we do and what we say.
2. We are morally responsible for the consequences of our choices.

The first principle goes back to what William Jennings Bryan said: your destiny is your choice. But what about when you feel powerless and out of control? We all feel this way at times—especially kids and teens.

Seeking good advice from people you trust is key to making sound decisions.

It's important to remember that having the power to make choices doesn't mean you have to make every choice alone. You also have the power to seek out good advice and to get the counsel of people you trust. So, part of making good choices is knowing how to get the help you need to make them.

The second principle is about understanding the full impact of the decisions you make. Every choice has a consequence—whether good or bad. And every choice affects certain people in some way. The people that are affected by a given choice are called "stakeholders." Most of us never even realize how many stakeholders there are for a given choice. Have you ever copied songs from a friend onto your MP3 player? Can you think of all the stakeholders affected by that choice? (Hint: It's not just you and the friend you copied from. Start thinking about the music download service, and the employees at the record company that sells the songs, and the musicians, producers, and engineers that work to create each song...).

So, thinking about all the stakeholders in a decision is one way to consider how important that decision is. It's another way of saying that the greater the consequence of a decision, the more important that decision is.

Okay, so now you know the principles of good decision-making. But the final part of the process is acting—actually making the ethical choice. Most of us know—most of the time—what the ethical choice is. The question is whether we *do it*—even if the consequences are costly to us or to others we care about.

Decision-Making Helpers

Choices are not always clear. Sometimes you will be pulled in many different directions as you consider what to do. Here are a few questions to ask yourself as you consider a decision. The answers may help to make the right choice clearer.

1. **Ask Yourself the Question of Universality**: If everyone made this choice, would it be a good thing?
2. **Ask Yourself the Golden Rule Question**: Would you want someone else to make this choice if it affected you the same way?
3. **Ask Yourself the Role Model Question**: Think of someone you know who is ethical and of strong character. What would that person do?

Building character is a lifelong process that takes courage, persistence, and strength.

Ethics Is Not for Wimps

Remember, being ethical is not always easy. It takes strength. And it often takes courage.

Being a person of strong character is not something that happens in a day or a week, or even years. For most "mere mortals," the strengthening of character is a lifelong process. There are always things to improve. Every year you work at it, your character will get better and better.

Ethical decisions can be difficult to make—and even more difficult to act upon. But great satisfaction and self-esteem come with knowing you did the right thing. Those positive feelings will inspire you to always make the right choices. This kind of satisfaction lasts a lifetime and brings you the most rewarding feeling of all: happiness.

Resources

WEB SITES:

CharacterCounts.org: The official site of CHARACTER COUNTS! provides information on programs, offers free resources and materials for students, parents, and teachers; also includes links to many other valuable and related sites.

Amnesty.org: The official site of Amnesty International, which works to end human rights abuses around the world.

Tolerance.org: Official web site of the organization that works to end hate crimes and violence around the world.

Stopcyberbullying.org; cyberbully411. org; cyberbully.us: All are web sites dedicated to providing statistics, information, and advice and to helping victims cope with bullying.

Lc2lc.org: Official web site of Loose Change to Loosen Chains, which works to stop slavery and human rights abuses around the world.

NOTABLE BOOKS ABOUT RESPECT:

Iggies House by Judy Blume: published by Atheneum, 2002.

Keystone Kids by John R. Tunis: published by Odyssey Classics, 2006.

The Sixth Grade Nickname Game by Gordon Korman: published by Hyperion, 2004.

Taking Sides by Gary Soto: published by Harcourt, 2003.

The Pistachio Prescription by Paula Danziger: published by Puffin, 2006.

The Bully by Anne E. Schraff: published by Scholastic, 2007.

Glossary

Cyberbullying: the use of technology, such as the Internet or text messaging, to cause harm to someone else.

Ethics: guidelines about right and wrong

Icon: an object that represents something important

Inhumane: cruel

Integrity: knowing and acting on what is right

Prejudice: unfair judgment against others

Stakeholders: people affected by a decision

Universality: applied to everyone

Index

Photo Credits